The author can be contacted at

hello@kcpediredla.com

Edition 1 - February 2024.

www.kcpediredla.com

ACKNOWLEDGEMENTS

This book could not be possible without my Grandmother and her blessings.

My wife Harika Pediredla, has always pushed me to do what I love and complete this book.

My two daughters Driti and Diviksha give me the inspiration to write and share my experiences in life.

My father, mother and brother, who have always supported me and helped me through my life in every phase.

INTRODUCTION

Companies (remote, hybrid, or office only) have much information that they generate for internal or external requirements. This information is stored in documents (PDFs, spreadsheets, presentations, word documents or any other document) and shared across the company and with external users like vendors, clients, contractors, etc.

Over the years of business operations, these documents (often stored on cloud platforms) get duplicated, copied, lost and even deleted. This makes creating, storing and retrieving information a challenging task for individuals within the business.

In this guide, I will attempt to put together a document management process with some examples to enable business leaders to plan their document management in a well-maintained and accessible manner, ensuring that individuals within the business are spending more time being productive and not duplicating or searching for information which is already available within the company.

WHAT IS DOCUMENT MANAGEMENT PROCESS?

Document management process is the process of systematically storing information in the form of documents. It's not rocket science, but every business struggles with this primarily because they do not have a documented process around it.

By the time they realise that they have lost or are unable to find information due to the lack of a proper document management process, it is too late, and most businesses lose a tonne of data and time due to this.

The process is set in place to guide individuals (including contractors, vendors and sometimes even clients) on properly handling documents. This includes how to name them, where to store them, and how to use them in an efficient way.

WHY IS THE DOCUMENT MANAGEMENT PROCESS NECESSARY?

I have run multiple businesses over the past 15 year. Over the tenure of running these companies, we generated many documents for various purposes like HR, Sales, Marketing and other business functions.

As team members joined and left each company over the years, many documents were created, shared, downloaded, and duplicated. We lost many of those documents because we did not take the time to understand the kind of information that each of those ex-employees had with them.

Some companies offer their team members company-owned devices, which can be taken back and processed correctly when the individual leaves the company. On the other hand, we had a combination of personal devices owned by the individual and rental devices rented out by the company for the team members to use.

This meant we had to either return devices with a quick wipe before handing the device over to the next employee or the vendor. When this happened, if the offboarding was done well, then we would take a backup before deleting all the data and dump it in a shared drive (which again led to more confusion and chaos due to the new arrival of unorganised documents), or if the offboarding was not done well, then it meant a clean wipe before realising that there might be some valuable data on those devices.

When it comes to personal devices, we had minimal control, which meant that when the individual leaves the company, we have no alternative but to trust their word and maybe a quick check if they did remove all the data and share it appropriately with the company.

The same situation occurs when new individuals join document-heavy departments like HR or Finance. Individuals tend to create, copy or edit many documents, which are usually shared with other team members or other vendors regularly (based on requirements). This usually means many copies of same documents are created and stored in random places.

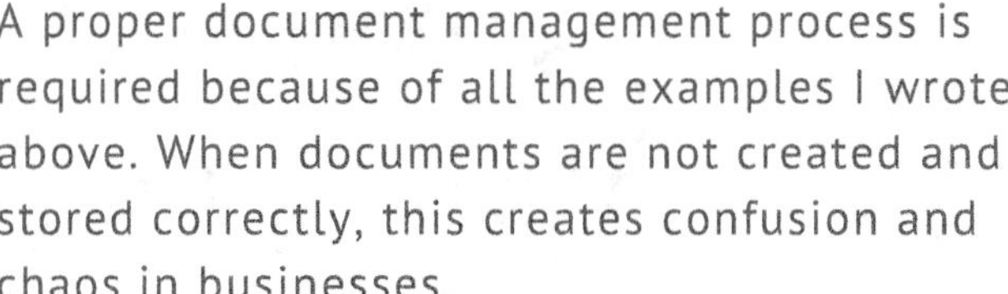

A proper document management process is required because of all the examples I wrote above. When documents are not created and stored correctly, this creates confusion and chaos in businesses.

We have all had that feeling at work where you want access to some information, be it a contract, a sales pitch, marketing material or an invoice, and you cannot seem to find it. You end up asking someone in any of these departments, and they spend hours tracking this document or creating a brand new one from scratch. This results in a loss of productive time and the creation of more records, which wastes device and cloud space for everyone.

COMPANIES NEED A PROPER PROCESS TO EXPLAIN HOW DOCUMENTS SHOULD BE MANAGED.

HOW SHOULD YOU CREATE A DOCUMENT MANAGEMENT PROCESS?

The process or steps involved in creating a document management process will be unique to each business. I can offer a guideline based on my experience managing documents across multiple companies in multiple countries. This can help you determine how to create the best document management process for your business.

Choosing the tool.

The first and most significant step for you will be to identify which platform or tool you will use for your document management process

.There are quite a few in the market, and choosing the tool will depend on multiple factors like pricing, features, security, accessibility, etc.

The usual ones in the market that most businesses work with are:
- Google Drive
- Microsoft One Drive
- Dropbox
- Box
- Zoho Drive
- iCloud (Maybe?)

MANY MORE PLATFORMS LIKE THOSE ENABLE BUSINESSES TO STORE, ACCESS AND MANAGE THEIR INTERNAL DOCUMENTATION.

The choice of tool doesn't make a big difference; it's more critical for you and your team members to be comfortable with the tool you decide to use. Just ensure that your subscription tier allows you access to shared folders.

For example, Google has shared folders accessible to everyone assigned to a department, but this feature is unavailable in the Business Basic subscription. The user must sign up for one of the other three subscription options to access this.

Do not worry if you feel like you have chosen the wrong tool. Most tools will allow you to take a backup, and then you can easily set this up in another tool you might want to use in future.

Identifying the high-level structure of document management.

Once you have identified the tool you want to use, the next step is to plan a structure for your document management.

There are two ways to plan this:

1. To plan the structure based on the office locations (if your business has multiple locations or intends to have various places in the future)
2. To plan the structure based on the departments in the company.

Office locations based document management structure:

Suppose your business has or intends to have multiple locations (could be cities or countries). In that case, consider planning a high-level document management structure based on these locations.

While most businesses have standard documents used across the company, operational, legal, or even marketing information may be stored in documents particular to a particular location and may not be helpful to individuals in other places.

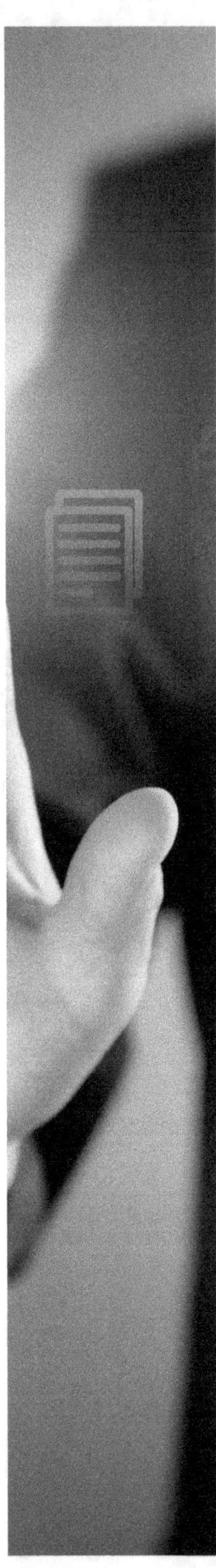

www.kcpediredla.com

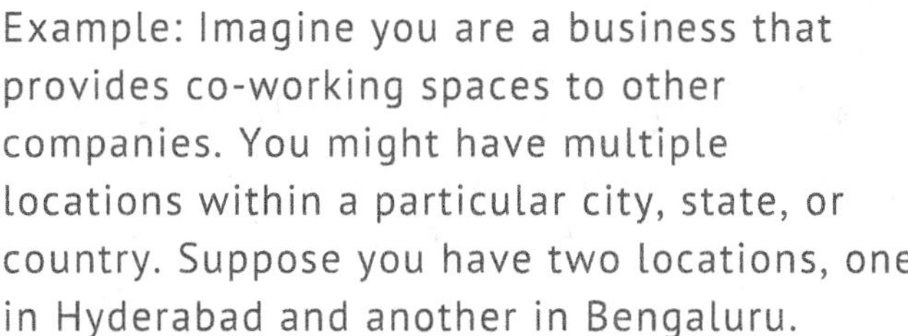

Example: Imagine you are a business that provides co-working spaces to other companies. You might have multiple locations within a particular city, state, or country. Suppose you have two locations, one in Hyderabad and another in Bengaluru.

If you store the documents in the following format:
- *Customers*
  - *Company D*
  - *Company M*
  - *Company S*

Then, it would be challenging to identify which customer belongs to which location. This makes it difficult for an individual within the company to quickly find details about a particular customer.

If you store the documents in the following format:
- *Hyderabad*
  - *Company D*
  - *Company M*
- *Bengaluru*
  - *Company S*
  - *Company G*

THIS MAKES IT EASIER FOR SOMEONE TO LEARN MORE ABOUT A CUSTOMER IN A PARTICULAR LOCATION.

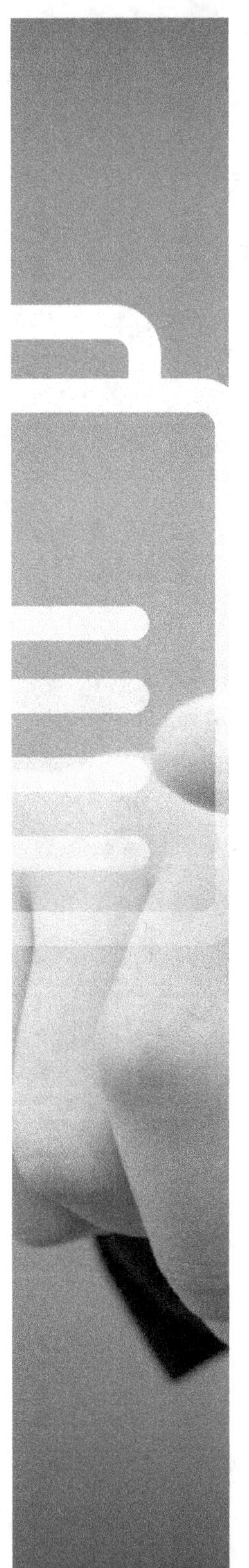

Arranging documents based on the office locations works well if each location's operations, finances, sales, or other business areas are handled separately for each site. This might work well in a franchised model, where each franchise owner is given some support, but each franchisee is responsible for effectively running a particular location.

Department-based document management structure:

Another way of managing documents in a business is to use departments as high-level folders and then use that folder to store all business documents related to a particular department.

This works well irrespective of having single or multiple locations if all the team members in the company report to the same department head (regardless of their location).

Example: Imagine you are part of a digital marketing team for a global SaaS-based product. You might have multiple locations and teams working on selling and managing the same product in every location.

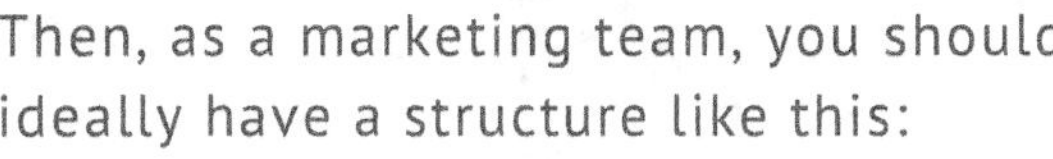

Then, as a marketing team, you should ideally have a structure like this:

- Marketing
  - Blogposts
    - Blog post 1
    - Blog post 2
    - Blog post 3
    - Blog post 4
  - Social Media Campaigns
    - Campaign 1
    - Campaign 2
    - Campaign 3
    - Campaign 4

Now, team members may write each blog post in different locations, and each campaign may target a different location or target audience. However, having all marketing campaigns in one place will ensure that the marketing department is aware of the work and can dip into the folders when they require content from a relevant campaign (irrespective of where it was run).

This model works well for owned businesses with multiple or only one location. They usually run one campaign across their locations or globally, so they do not need to segregate the information based on location. Hence, it is advisable to have a department-focused document management structure.

Create a Document Naming Convention:

We underestimate the importance of adequately naming a document. It works well when you are starting a business. Still, when you have to search for a particular contract or a template quickly, you realise that finding the proper document in the thousands of documents in your business drive can become messy.

You could run a quick search in your document management system to find the correct document, but what will you search for if you have no idea what it would have been saved as?

As someone with over fifteen years' worth of documents pulled in from multiple online and offline drives, finding so many "untitled" and "template" titled files is frustrating. It took me a few days to open each one, identify what they were and rename them appropriately. I can find most documents in my drive more easily now than before.

THINK OF SOMETHING LIKE <DEPARTMENT NAME>_<PURPOSE>_TEMPLATE OR SOMETHING THAT MAKES SENSE TO YOU AND YOUR BUSINESS WHEN CREATING A NAMING CONVENTION.

Once you decide on the naming convention, ensure that every document in the business follows this convention. This will help save so many hours for various team members in your business.

Define roles.

Each document in your business likely has multiple users who might open, print, or even edit it. However, one person or department is always responsible for the document; this needs to be defined at the initial stages of the document's creation.

This is why it is essential to understand the different roles and the level of access for each role in the document management system.

Here are a few common ones to remember and potentially use:

Owner:

This role in a business is almost always the business itself or the business owner. This could be an individual who is the director of the company or the management as a whole, who is responsible for running the business smoothly.

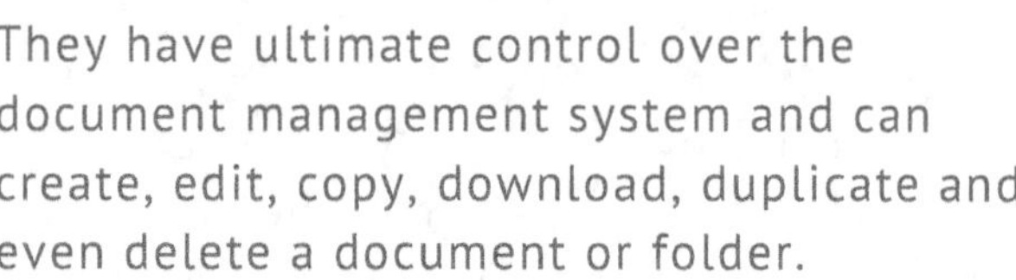

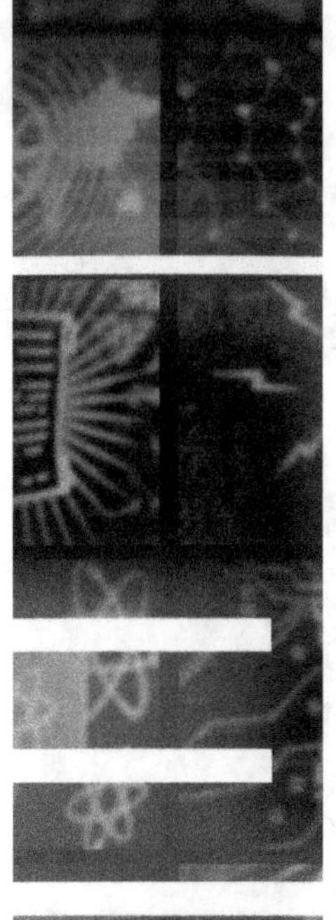

They have ultimate control over the document management system and can create, edit, copy, download, duplicate and even delete a document or folder.

Creator:

This role is usually automatically catered to the individual or team who creates a document in the document management system. They can be any individual within the organisation, employee, manager, or business owner.

If they are not the business owner, they usually have the control to create, edit, maybe copy, download and duplicate the document. Depending on the business rules and the amount of data security required, they may even be able to delete or not delete a document.

Editor:

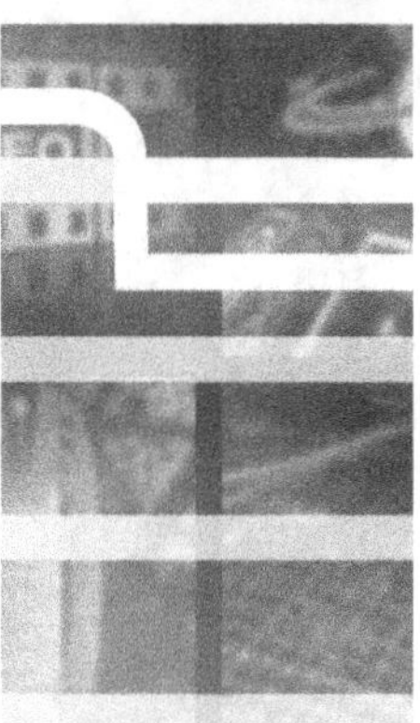

This role has to be assigned to an individual by the document's owner or the creator. The editor can be any individual within or outside the organisation (who might collaborate with the creator to work on the document).

The editor can make changes to the document and most likely copy or download the document as well. Depending on the editor's role in the document, they might even have access to delete it.

The right to delete a document should never be given to an editor outside the company. This ensures the business can retain that document's information for future use.

Commentor:

This role has to be assigned to an individual by the owner or creator of the document. The commenter usually collaborates on the document with the creator and can only provide their thoughts on various information in the document.

The commenter should ideally not be able to edit or delete the document.

Think about access control.

Information is essential these days, so having a proper access control plan and document management process is crucial.

Access control is something that a business should think about when putting together a document management process. There are two areas that companies should explore when thinking about this:

Shared or Collaborative Documents

It is common in large businesses to provide access to internal documents for individuals or companies who need access to that information at a given time and date. But once that purpose is fulfilled, most businesses and team members forget that someone else can still access this document.

If left unchecked, these individuals or companies have the opportunity to misuse the information in this document.

Hence, it becomes essential for businesses to have proper plans on:
- Who to provide access to?
- How long should the access be provided for?
- When should access be revoked for better security?

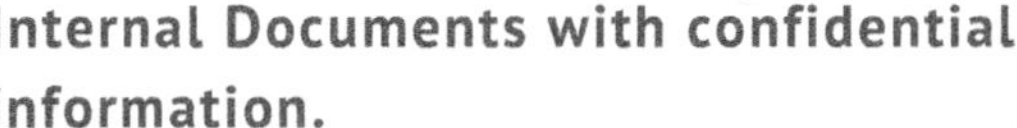

Internal Documents with confidential information.

Besides external documents, internal documents within an organisation are not for everyone in the team. It is also essential for the business to think about managing access control for these documents.

Think of something like a company strategy or even a department strategy for the coming year. It usually has many ideas on what can be done better in the next year in the draft versions. Within this document, there could be confidential information like salary changes, additions or removals of team members or even potential new services or products in the idea stage.

All of the information is very confidential and should not be shared with everyone in the business.

Due to the availability of sensitive information on these documents, the creator and owner should ensure that they are stored in locations that the rest of the team members in the business or other departments do not have access to.

Create contingency plans.

Documents are prone to getting deleted or corrupted for various reasons. This is even more true in the cloud-only world where we run our document management systems today.

We never know when a company hosting or saving the data belonging to your business is impacted by malware or a cyber attack or something.

That is why it is essential to choose the right tool for your document management system also it is even more critical to ensure that they have regular backups of your data.

Depending on the kind of data you as a business have access to and its importance for your business operations, it is advisable to have data backed up to external physical or third-party tools regularly.

WHO SHOULD BE CREATING THE DOCUMENT MANAGEMENT PROCESS?

Your company's document management process will potentially stay active till the end of your company tenure. This is why someone in management needs to be ideally responsible for creating the document management process.

It does not have to be the CEO, but it needs someone who understands the need and implements it from a place of authority to ensure that everyone in the company adopts it.

While the overall document management process needs to be set up from a higher level view of the business, each department needs to set up its own rules and best practices around how to name a document, how to save a document and who has access to it.

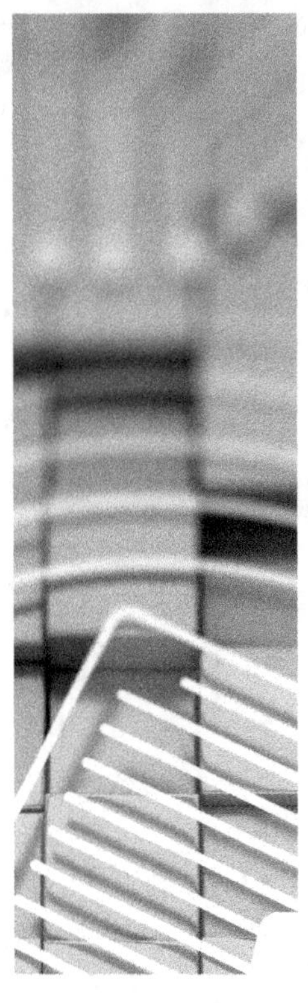

There should be clear guidelines on how each department shares and provides access to the documents to other departments.

If this is not planned and audited well, team members will likely lose track of all the documents and continue providing unnecessary access to individuals who no longer need a document. This scenario is very much seen in the HR department. By the nature of this department, they create many documents, which are then shared with other departments for various purposes. But later, they forget to revoke that access, which may no longer apply to different departments.

All of this must be considered when implementing the document management process.

As the business expands and has many employees, it can be delegated to the administrative department. This department is sometimes responsible for ensuring that all the data within the company is identified, stored, secured and shared with the correct set of people within and outside the organisation.

Ideally, multiple individuals should have access to and knowledge of the process within the organisation, but one individual or team should be responsible for executing the method.

www.kcpediredla.com

It is important that multiple individuals within an organisation know how to execute and implement the document management process.

This ensures that the process is continued within the business, even when the key individual who had set up the process at first leaves the business due to any reason.

WHEN SHOULD YOU CREATE A DOCUMENT MANAGEMENT PROCESS?

The simple answer to this question is - when you start your business. However, I understand that it is not the top priority for most business owners when they start a new business.

The focus is on just starting the business, hiring the right people, and getting sales, equipment, etc. But you, as a business owner, need to understand that even before you start all of this, you begin accumulating digital items like registration certificates, tax documents, company letterheads, bills, etc.

These documents need to be saved somewhere where they are not just accessible to you but also to your future team members in different departments who might have to use these documents or review them for any specific purpose.

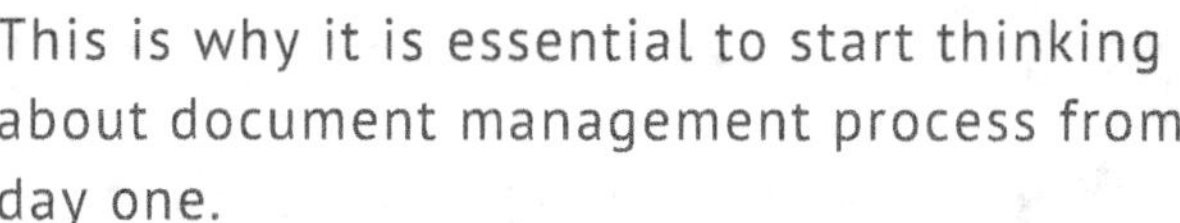

This is why it is essential to start thinking about document management process from day one.

As you grow as a business and start bringing in new departments and locations, it becomes essential to have areas where these new departments or locations can save documents related to their department or location.

I have already discussed how to do this in the "How should you create a document management process" section above in this book.

HOW TO CONDUCT A DOCUMENT REVIEW FOR YOUR BUSINESS?

If you have not yet implemented the Document Management Process in your business and it's been a few years since you have started a business. Then, it might sound like a challenging task to undertake.

But believe me, it is very much needed for every business. If you are looking to implement a document management process, here is how you can do it:

Create a master folder or drive:

The first big task is to create a shared folder or drive where all your company documents can be moved.

Identify a structure:

This has been explained already in this ebook, but once you select a master folder or drive, create a structure at a higher level. This could be location or department.

You can either spend more time and create the whole structure for each area like:
- Finances
  - Invoices
  - Bills
  - Financial Statements
  - Budgets

Or, you can create a master folder called "Finances".

Dump the documents:

Once you have created the structure, you can dump all the files you can access in their folders. If it's a master folder, you can dump all of them in the master folder, or if you have created the whole structure, you can drop each document in its specific folder.

Collect all documents:

Once you have dumped all the documents in your folder, talk to your team members across the business to ensure that they dump all the documents regarding the company in these folders.

This should become the one source of all documents in your business, Making it easy to find any document and information when needed.

Rename the documents:

Once you dump all the files in their respective folders, you need to look at renaming them in accordance with a convention. This will help you find your documents more efficiently.

Review access to documents:

Once you have collected and renamed these documents, run a quick check to see who still has access to these documents. Check if they still need access to this document or not and remove access where needed.

Delete obsolete documents:

The final step is to clear the excess. Delete any old or useless documents. During the dump and cleanup process, you will likely find duplicates; I have noticed that many businesses have the same file saved across different devices and with various individuals.

These documents get shared across teams and create many duplicates within the business. It is essential to delete them to ensure that there is only one source of documents and information for the company.

CONCLUSION

Document management is one of the most overlooked processes in a business. Businesses only realise the importance of it when conducting an audit or when someone needs a particular file but cannot find it in time.

Use this ebook to implement the document management process within your business, and reach out to hello@kcpediredla.com if you have any questions on how to implement this better.

9 798882 819292